The ART OF WRITING

Four Principles for Great Writing that Everyone Needs to Know

Peter Yang

TCK
PUBLISHING.COM

Copyright © 2019 by Peter Yang.

All Rights Reserved.

No part of this publication may be reproduced, distributed, or transmitted in any form or by any means, including photocopying, recording, or other electronic or mechanical methods, or by any information storage and retrieval system without the prior written permission of the publisher, except in the case of very brief quotations embodied in critical reviews and certain other noncommercial uses permitted by copyright law.

ISBN: 978-1-63161-076-9

Sign up for Peter Yang's newsletter at
www.peteryangauthor.com/free

Published by TCK Publishing
www.TCKpublishing.com

Get discounts and special deals
on our best selling books at
www.TCKpublishing.com/bookdeals

Check out additional discounts for bulk orders at
www.TCKpublishing.com/bulk-book-orders

CONTENTS

INTRODUCTION	*vii*
PRINCIPLE 1: Economy	*1*
Crush Your Crutches	*5*
Don't Repeat Yourself	*6*
Write with Conviction	*7*
Streamline Your Writing	*8*
Remove Unnecessary Cases of *Which* Is and *That*	*10*
Write in the Positive	*12*
Be Judicious with the Information You Provide	*13*
Use Punctuation Sparingly	*16*
Prefer the Active Voice tothe Passive Voice	*17*
PRINCIPLE 2: Transparency	*21*
Be Intentional	*23*
Use Figures of SpeechYour Readers Understand	*25*
Write to the Layman	*26*
Avoid Clichés	*27*
Stick to One Interpretation	*27*
Create Sharp Distinctions	*29*
Describe with Purpose	*30*
Make Your Tense Shifts Deliberate	*31*

Be Meticulous with Your Modifiers	*33*
Make *This* Clear	*35*
Prefer the Concrete to the Abstract	*37*
Avoid Flowery Language	*38*
Save the Best for Last	*39*
PRINCIPLE 3: Variety	*43*
Vary Your Sentence Structures	*45*
Vary Your Paragraph Structures	*47*
Vary Your Word Choice	*51*
PRINCIPLE 4: Harmony	*55*
Harmonize Your Language	*58*
Harmonize Your Thoughts	*63*
Say What You Mean and Mean What You Say	*67*
CODA: Meditations on Writing	*69*
Reading to Write	*71*
Is There Objectively Good Writing?	*73*
Time as a Valuable Resource	*74*
Writing as Autobiography	*77*
The Error of Arrogance	*80*
Truth—the Cornerstone of Artistic Writing	*81*
ABOUT THE AUTHOR	85
CONNECT WITH PETER	89

For my loving family,
whose undying support continues to surprise me.

INTRODUCTION

SOME TIME AGO, I WAS prompted by a friend to write down what I believed were the ten most important skills every person needed to develop to live a fulfilled life. An innately curious and abstract thinker, he was trying to establish the axioms on which human success was built. He proposed that if he could determine these fundamental skills, he could come to better his life and the lives of those around him.

I was intrigued by the mysterious nature of his question. So, I proceeded with his request, jotting a few details down on a sheet of paper and ranking the skills from most to least important.

The next day, my friend called me, saying, "Hey, I thought you were a writer. Why didn't you include writing on the list?" I was speechless, and he was right. After all, I was a writer, and writing was extremely important to me. While I was quick to mention the necessity of being able to play a musical instrument or negotiate a tough deal, I had taken writing for granted. In fact, it never crossed my mind that writing was a skill at all!

For many people, writing is not something to be *actively improved upon*. Rather, upon reaching a certain level of literacy, many feel they can safely assert: Look at me, I can write now! Many university graduates will write at the same level of literacy for the rest of their lives, not thinking that perhaps what they're saying could be more concise, more *precise*. And for the same reason—that is, because I didn't see the ability to write as something that needed to be constantly honed and refined—I failed to see writing as a fundamental life skill.

In many ways, that moment became the catalyst for *The Art of Writing*. It encouraged me to think about the importance of writing on the individual and broader society. It forced me to consider a world without writing—a world, no doubt, characterized by chaos and ignorance. It made me realize that writing was something you should become *skillful* at.

I began noticing how an author's writing style directly influenced the allure of an idea, irrespective of the value of the idea itself! I observed how writing with clarity and passion could make a work *that much more* effective and compelling. It soon became clear: Writing was not merely a fundamental skill, but an artistic pursuit!

I encourage you to write your own list, high-lighting your take on the ten most important life skills. Ask yourself: How much do you value the ability to write well? How would becoming a better writer improve your career? Your life? If you're a student, how might it influence your studies?

There is an emerging belief that writing is simply becoming obsolete (at least, the ability to write clearly and coherently). Why write in complete sentences when "internet speak" can be used to convey the same message in fewer words? Why go through the trouble of learning how to properly spell when autocorrection has become so prevalent and increasingly accurate? What has made the pursuit of elegant writing so unpopular and feared? Why are people still struggling with distinguishing *there*, *their*, and *they're*?

Perhaps all these questions can be addressed through one general question: *Why don't people like to write?*

Because *writing is difficult*. But as with all challenging pursuits, I assure you that writing well is worth the effort it takes.

Think of writing as more than just an activity. Think of it as an art form insofar as it is, according to the Oxford English Dictionary, "the expression and application of human creative skill and imagination." Writing must be considered not through the lenses of strict scientific analysis, but through the lenses of an interpreter of art. It is, ultimately, an artistic pursuit, and should be treated as such, whether your end goal is to create a true work of art or simply a well-crafted email.

Let me be clear: Everyone can be a writer, if they so choose. What you write is not important—writers can write novels, technical manuals, poetry, journal entries, or scientific papers. To be a writer, you simply need to write.

Artistic writing, in this broad sense, consists of four fundamental principles: economy, transparency, variety, and harmony. These principles serve as a necessary foundation for anyone wanting to enrich their writing, which will, in turn, enrich their life.

Like visual art, artistic writing is colorful and individualistic. It embodies the character and spirit of the writer, and is elegant, compelling, and unique in style. It does not beg to be heard nor does it desire to be heard by the apathetic slob. Artistic writing is writing that does not attempt to impress; rather, it is writing that attempts to communicate. Artistic writing is a conversation, not a lecture: It invites the reader to meditate on what is being said, not to superficially understand it.

Artistic writing is not strictly a means to an end, but an end in itself. It is a joyous activity, and it is the personal fulfillment that comes with artistic writing that has made it so deeply rooted in our culture.

There is an artistic writer in all of us; to tap into it, you need simply to unleash your dormant but ever-present artistic potential. It is simply the lack of motivation and strategy that separates artistic writing from unartistic writing.

There are five central attributes that distinguish every artistic writer:

I) **Artistic writers are *meticulous* in their work.** They ask of every word, "Is this necessary? Could my writing do without it?"

II) **Artistic writers are *cognizant* of their audience's values.** They know who their readers are and what they stand for. They write not *to* the readers, but *for* the readers.

III) **Artistic writers are *sincere* to their readers.** They do not lie out of fear but testify out of courage. They ensure that rhetoric never stands in the way of communication and that their desire for acclaim never stands in the way of truth.

IV) **Artistic writers are not obsessed with perfection.** They acknowledge that perfection is a pointless and unattainable goal.

V) **Artistic writers are *flexible* with the four principles.** They know that the principles in this book should always be weighed in the context of what they're writing.

Anyone can learn to write artistically. It is my hope that the four principles laid out in these pages will help guide you along the path to becoming an artistic writer.

PRINCIPLE 1

ECONOMY

Economy is a matter of using the fewest words to produce the most meaning. It is often the excess of words and ideas, not the lack of them, that dilutes the power of your writing. The composition of your writing should imitate the anatomy of a flower—every part should be necessary and contribute to the whole. Any words that can be cut out must be cut out, and any sentences that can be shortened must be shortened. Ask ruthlessly of every sentence, "Can I express this more simply?" Continue until you've reached a point where you have stripped away everything but the essentials.

A sentence is like a mathematical expression: The more it can be simplified, the more beautiful it becomes. There is nothing more fundamental to the artistic writer's philosophy.

When simplifying a sentence, it helps to follow a methodical process similar to mathematical proofing. When mathematicians approach an equation, they attempt to solve it one step at a time, showing all their work in a logical, descending sequence. By applying the same technique, writers can take a structured approach to artistic writing.

It goes without saying that one's reading has a strong influence on one's writing.

~~It goes without saying that~~ one's reading has a strong influence on one's writing.

~~One's~~ reading has a strong influence on ~~one's~~ writing.

Reading has a strong influence on writing.

Reading strongly influences writing.

The evidence is definitely not irrefutable.

The evidence is ~~definitely~~ not irrefutable.

The evidence is not irrefutable.

The evidence is refutable.

It is impossible for him to stop repeating that message over and over again.

He cannot stop repeating that message ~~over and over again~~.

He cannot stop repeating that message.

Prefer the shorter word to the longer word, the shorter sentence to the longer sentence, and the shorter paragraph to the longer paragraph. To ramble senselessly is a pretentious waste of the reader's time.

But make no mistake: To exchange meaning for brevity is no better. Concise prose alone is insufficient. If more words are required to express an idea, then more words should be used.

Crush Your Crutches

Crutch words commonly manifest themselves in spoken English. Sometimes called "filler words," crutch words are meaningless parcels of language that writers and speakers alike tend to inadvertently pepper across every sentence. They have become a monumental problem in our age of volubility and must be avoided if economy is to be achieved.

You might argue, "But to write with crutch words is to write naturally! By removing crutch words, wouldn't I be removing my individuality?" Artistic writers should be able to express themselves without the need for filler language. To write naturally is not to write carelessly, but to write in a way that best reflects your values, aspirations, and ideals. Crutch words rarely clarify or improve your writing, nor do they facilitate expression.

Jaxon would **definitely** never do that.
Jaxon would never do that.

Macy **actually** didn't know what was happening.
Macy didn't know what was happening.

Richard **literally** never got tired of playing hockey.
Richard never got tired of playing hockey.

Don't Repeat Yourself

A tautology is an unnecessary (and often unintentional) repetition of meaning. Tautologies, if not for rhetorical effect, must be avoided. They have no place in artistic writing.

He was met with an **unexpected surprise**.
He was met with a surprise.

Perhaps it will forever remain an **unsolved mystery**.

Perhaps it will forever remain a mystery.

It is estimated that two out of every one hundred people, or 2% of the world population, has green eyes.

It is estimated that 2% of the world population has green eyes.

Write with Conviction

Qualifiers are words or phrases whose purpose is to limit or enhance an adjective or adverb's meaning.

When used sparingly, qualifiers can improve the quality and precision of your message. However, qualifiers are often abused in writing, strewn across every sentence with the hope of creating a more nuanced piece of work. Rather, the inclusion of too many qualifiers is the ultimate token of the immature writer and signals a lack of conviction. Use qualifiers only when strictly necessary!

It was a **rather** sunny day.

It was a sunny day.

He was **quite** tired.

He was tired.

If you think a qualifier is necessary for emphatic reasons, it may be better to change the qualified word entirely.

The dessert was **very** tasty.

The dessert was scrumptious.

Streamline Your Writing

Transition words create bridges between ideas in your writing, linking them together and strengthening their connections. These words are useful but must be employed heedfully and skillfully. When used unnecessarily, transition words become pointless flourishes. Thus, writers should try to streamline their writing in such a way that each sentence leads naturally to the next, eliminating the need for transition words in most cases.

A recent study shows that millennials, on average, check their phones 150 times per day. **Furthermore,** the same publication reveals that 17% of millennials check their phones during sex.

A recent study shows that millennials, on average, check their phones 150 times per day. The same publication reveals that 17% of millennials check their phones during sex.

Although writing is hard, mastery can be achieved with structured practice. **Therefore**, by consistently trying to improve your writing, you will become a better writer.

Mastery in writing can be achieved with structured practice. By consistently trying to improve your writing, you will become a better writer.

An outline is an essential part of the writing process. **Nevertheless**, it is one that many writers overlook. **More accurately**, it is one that many writers ignore.

An outline is an essential part of the writing process that many writers ignore.

Remove Unnecessary Cases of *Which Is* and *That*

The phrase *which is* is frequently unnecessary and can often be omitted from a sentence without sacrificing any meaning.

Katherine hates shopping during the Christmas season, **which is** the busiest shopping season of the year.

Katherine hates shopping during the Christmas season, the busiest shopping season of the year.

Paul's favorite toy, **which is** a teddy bear, is beginning to fall apart.

Paul's favorite toy, a teddy bear, is beginning to fall apart.

Jose hasn't been exercising lately, **which is** one reason he's beginning to gain weight.

Jose hasn't been exercising lately—one reason he's beginning to gain weight.

That is another word sprinkled recklessly and unnecessarily over many pieces of writing. It is a writer's nightmare to find every unnecessary instance of *that* after completing a work. Therefore, it's best to monitor your usage as you write.

Matt was surprised **that** Olivia agreed to dance with him.

Matt was surprised Olivia agreed to dance with him.

The word *that* is abused so often **that** it eventually becomes an annoyance.

The word *that* is abused so often it eventually becomes an annoyance.

It is unreasonable to believe **that** books have souls.

It is unreasonable to believe books have souls.

Write in the Positive

Double negatives force your readers to uncoil otherwise simple sentences. Remember: Two negatives make a positive. Keep in mind, however, that double negatives often have a place in poetry and rhetoric.

It **wasn't** that Sam **didn't** care about school. He just didn't enjoy it.

Sam cared about school but didn't enjoy it.

Katherine was **not unconvinced** by his argument.

Katherine was convinced by his argument.

It was **not uncommon** for James to smoke a cigarette after work.

It was common for James to smoke a cigarette after work.

There **never** went a day when Joseph did **not** miss her.

Joseph always missed her.

Be Judicious with the Information You Provide to Your Readers

Writers are often afraid they haven't written enough. However, it is more typically the case that the writer has done too much, written too much. This issue is so prevalent that writers have even coined a term for it: *info dump*.

In info dumps, writers have taken every chance to coat their writing with senseless baggage that does nothing to enhance their message. In doing so, they have done the reader a disservice.

"So, we're going on a road trip? Last time we attempted this, we ended up lost in the middle of nowhere for two days straight!" Cathy exclaimed. "I'm not going with you again, Jenna. You almost got both of us killed. And it was on my birthday, too!"

Two hours and twenty-five minutes later, Harry walked through the wooden front door, which had been painted bright red and had two small square windows at the top. He paused for a moment to look at his front yard. To his left were four lilac bushes that had been planted by the previous owners of the house. They looked wilted, almost ugly, and there were only two purplish-blue flowers between all of the plants. On the right was a patch of sad-looking brown dirt, since grass seemingly refused to grow there.

Crime rates are rising in metropolitan areas. Thankfully, rural areas seem to be doing just fine. As this trend continues, cities will have to invest more heavily in law enforcement.

Artistic writers have self-restraint and humility that allows them to tailor the amount of information they provide to their specific audience. They weigh the importance of what they write in relation to their audience's values, not their own.

It is the author's responsibility to explain that, and only that, which is fundamental to their case. Tangents, while sometimes fun and interesting, will inevitably distract readers and, therefore, dilute your overall argument. Ask yourself: Is this sentence bringing the reader closer to understanding my point, if only incrementally? If the answer is no, it has no place in your writing.

In fiction specifically, it is the author's responsibility to find the right balance between explanation and description. Fully imagined characters, of course, have lives before the story begins—a sixteen-year-old girl wasn't suddenly birthed at the start of the narrative. So, frantically, the author tries to bring their readers up to speed about all sixteen years— on page one. But even attempts at subtlety—such as manifesting her life experiences in dialogue with a friend—end up obvious and forced.

By exposing too much information, they strip their narrative of the ability to develop and their reader of the chance to understand the story in an organic way.

Authors should say enough to strike an image in the reader's mind, but not say so much that imagination is irrelevant. By writing too much, authors may trap their readers into *their* perception of the story. This defies the fundamental premise of storytelling—the creative freedom that comes with taking a story and making it your own. The art of storytelling lies not in your ability to tell, but in your ability to withhold.

Use Punctuation Sparingly

Writers must be economical in more than their use of words, for words are only the building blocks of language. Writers must also be economical in their use of punctuation.

Like words, punctuation marks must be used sparingly and only when strictly necessary. Humans can only account for so much information at a time. The more commas and semicolons you include in a sentence, the more knots you're forcing the reader to unwind to grasp your message. Limit the number of punctuation marks in your writing for a cleaner, more effective piece of prose.

Jonathan didn't like reading; he thought it was a waste of time.

Jonathan didn't like reading because he thought it was a waste of time.

Melody wanted to be either of two things: a nurse, or a dentist.

Melody wanted to be either a nurse or a dentist.

It soon became clear: Gary wasn't his friend anymore.

It soon became clear Gary wasn't his friend anymore.

Prefer the Active Voice to the Passive Voice

As a rule of thumb, use the active voice for a cleaner, more powerful message.

What Is the Active Voice?

The active voice is direct and vigorous. In the active voice, the subject of a sentence performs the action.

Martha kissed Gordon.

The police are performing an investigation.

The man waved to the little girl.

What Is the Passive Voice?

The passive voice is the active voice's shy sister. In the passive voice, the subject receives the action.

Gordon was kissed by Martha.

An investigation is being performed by the police.

The little girl was waved to by the man.

When to Use Active Voice and Passive Voice

The active voice brings a sense of control and forcefulness to your writing. For this reason, it is often preferred in day-to-day writing and in journalism. The active voice is best used when answering a question, addressing an issue, or whenever candidness is your top priority.

(Active) I didn't eat breakfast yesterday.

(Passive) Breakfast was not eaten by me yesterday.

(Active) The child did not pull the fire alarm.

(Passive) The fire alarm was not pulled by the child.

(Active) Randy didn't enjoy Sunday mornings.

(Passive) Sunday mornings were not enjoyed by Randy.

However, some writers make the mistake of avoiding the passive voice altogether. Doing this will make your writing sound monotonous, prescriptive, and downright awkward. Do not be afraid to use the passive voice, for one voice is not decisively better than the other.

The passive voice is best used when the writer wants to emphasize the *recipient* of the action, not the performer of the action.

(Passive) This **house** was built by my grandfather.

(Active) My grandfather built this house.

(Passive) The **building** was engulfed by a fire.

(Active) Fire engulfed the building.

(Passive) The **ball** was caught by Tony.

(Active) Tony caught the ball.

ered by Anna’s Archive (annas-archive.org), mirror of Library Genesis
PRINCIPLE 2

TRANSPARENCY

Transparent writing is writing that is lucid and explicit. It leaves no room for doubt and assures the intelligibility of your ideas. A writer's work can hew to the other three principles but fail to be artistic if it does not conform to the principle of transparency. Writing that lacks transparency does not have meaning. Therefore, make sure that everything you write is written with the utmost transparency.

Be Intentional

Bland writing often stems from a lack of clear intentions. The most common plight of everyday writers is the absence of foresight: the ability of writers to develop a sharp mental image of what they are going to write before doing so. Many writers do not take the time to *think*. Instead, they prefer to just *do*. Ironically, these writers often ask themselves in the writing process, "Why can't I think of something to write? Why have I come to a sudden impasse?"

Too many writers overlook the most pivotal step in the crafting of a beautifully written piece: planning! Planning is the bedrock of all great writing. To not plan your writing is analogous to building a ship without a blueprint, drawing a portrait without an outline, or shooting a movie without a script: The final product will be an unequivocal mess.

Do not be the fool who dismisses a comprehensive outline or constructs one only out of sheer necessity. It is often more challenging to devise an intricate outline of a piece of writing than it is to write it.

Form a habit of planning your pieces, if only for five to ten minutes. Ask yourself what justifies your writing's existence. Once you know *why* you're writing something, it becomes much easier to know *how* you're going to write it.

In doing these things, you will find that your writing becomes more engaging, you will find an instant upsurge in the quality and transparency of your writing, and you will find that your writing is more *structured* and *beautiful.*

Use Figures of Speech Your Readers Understand

Figurative language is the representation of one thing in terms of another to promote understanding of abstract or high-level concepts. Many different types of figurative language exist, but they all serve this purpose. The most recognized type is the metaphor. For example: A writer paints pictures with words.

When used properly, figures of speech can greatly illuminate your writing. However, be wary of overloading your writing with analogies. When you analogize, you force the reader to see past the literal. If overused, however, figurative language can undermine the effectiveness of your message.

When speaking in the non-literal, particularly if this manifests itself as a series of figurative statements, make sure everything you say is contextually appropriate and understandable, both in relation to your topic and in relation to your audience's intellect and interests.

Write to the Layman

Jargon is technical language that is used only in reference to a specialized topic. If you're writing for a general audience—an audience unfamiliar with the literature and technicalities surrounding your topic—it is best to eliminate any jargon from your work. Unless you're writing an esoteric treatise for a clique of specialists or academics, jargon is empty, often pretentious language that precludes transparency in your writing.

If it is imperative that you use jargon, make sure to define it within the context of what you're saying.

Forte is a musical term indicating that music is to be played loudly.

UX is an abbreviation of "user experience," referring to a person's experience using a particular product in terms of its ease of use, etc.

Left-wing is a political term describing a person with a liberal viewpoint.

Avoid Clichés

Clichés are phrases that have lost their charm due to overuse. Many writers contend with a subconscious urge to scatter clichés in their writing. This inevitably makes their writing appear unoriginal, uninspiring, and lazy. Clichés are expedient but show a lack of creative thought. Whenever one presents itself in your writing, strike it out with the utmost force and readiness.

Laughter is the best medicine.

Don't judge a book by its cover.

Easier said than done.

Stick to One Interpretation

Ambiguity is the possibility that a word, phrase, or sentence is open to several plausible interpretations in a given context. It is easy to see how ambiguity stands in the way of transparency, as it can lead the reader to believe something entirely different from what the writer intended.

Writers are often not aware that what they're saying could be ambiguous. They have a mental image of what it is they are trying to express and take for granted that the reader will have the same. Remember: Just because you know what you mean does not imply that the reader will necessarily know what you mean.

To identify ambiguities, you could try to look at your writing from the perspective of a first-time reader, but this can be a nearly impossible task. The best, and perhaps only, method to reliably pinpoint ambiguities in your writing is by giving it to someone else to read. In the case that this is not a viable option, take a break from your writing and come back to it a few days later (at the very least).

While ambiguity may find its appeal in poetry and fictional dialogue, there is no excuse for ambiguous writing in the realm of informative prose.

The rivalry between Johnathan and Adam has intensified since his promotion to COO.

(Who got promoted?)

Isaac found a bat in his backyard.

(Is the bat an animal or a piece of sports equipment—and whose backyard is it?)

The cat chased the mouse until it could no longer run.

(Who could no longer run?)

Create Sharp Distinctions

Artistic writing makes sharp contrasts between opposing ideas. The sharper the contrast, the more vivid the distinction, and the more powerful and transparent the writing.

When making a distinction, use diametrically opposed words to establish the greatest possible contrast. This juxtaposition will ensure that the reader acknowledges and understands the polarity between your ideas.

Jerry hated swimming; Martha quite enjoyed swimming.

Jerry **hated** swimming; Martha **loved** swimming.

Courtney was bright, whereas her brother was clumsy.

Courtney was **bright**, whereas her brother was **dull**.

Zackery was always extroverted, whereas Bethany always preferred being alone.

Zackery was always **extroverted**, whereas Bethany was always **introverted**.

Describe with Purpose

When using descriptive language, make sure you are not repeating yourself with adjectives that are too similar in meaning. Redundant adjectives are boring and serve no purpose.

The statue was beautiful, gorgeous, and ravishing.

The manager was hideous, ugly, and unsightly.

The child felt petrified, scared, and alarmed.

Every adjective you use should elicit a different feeling in the reader's mind. Some adjectives may have similar meanings but different connotations, as in the following example.

Fred was clever, knowledgeable, and wise.

Although the adjectives have related meanings, they each express a distinct idea. Together, they create a more complete description than any one alone.

Make Your Tense Shifts Deliberate

Unmotivated tense shifting throughout your writing confuses the reader and makes your writing ungraceful. It undermines flow and has a jarring effect.

This is not to say that shifting tenses is strictly forbidden. Writers will sometimes shift from past tense to present tense to add to the vividness of a narrative account. In a story, the author may switch to the present tense for immersive effect if a character is experiencing a flashback. In a report, the author may switch to the present tense when relaying a personal anecdote. These are accepted and powerful ways of enhancing the punch of your message.

Therefore, if you switch between tenses throughout your writing, make sure there is always a justified motivation behind it and that it takes place at an appropriate time. Never shift tenses midsentence or midparagraph. Always wait for a break in the writing (perhaps a section or chapter) before doing so.

(Multiple tenses) George said he won't go to the celebration, knowing it will be the final chance for him to bid Chloe farewell before she departed for New York.

(Single tense) George said he wouldn't go to the celebration, knowing it would be the final chance for him to bid Chloe farewell before she left for New York.

Be Meticulous with Your Modifiers

Modifiers are words, phrases, or clauses that give supplementary information about, or *modify*, another word or word group.

Modifiers are often misplaced in sentences, leading to unwanted nuances in meaning. While these typically go unnoticed, some misplaced modifiers can have substantial consequences.

Michael had a **warm bowl** of tomato soup for dinner.

Michael had a bowl of **warm tomato soup** for dinner.

The two friends ate the food they had **cooked slowly**.

The two friends **slowly ate** the food they had cooked.

This is particularly relevant when a writer is referring to two different things but using only one modifier. Often, a writer will want to modify one word but inadvertently modifies both by placing the modifier *before* both words. This is easily fixed by changing the order of the sentence.

William enjoyed lazily watching TV and exercising.

William enjoyed exercising and **lazily watching TV.**

Stop Making the Reader Do Arithmetic

Especially common in journalism, fractions and ratios force readers to perform mental arithmetic. Writers who use them overlook the fact that not all readers are mathematicians.

It can be fruitless and annoying for readers to have to process an intimidating mathematical fraction describing the probability for a decline in gas prices. Thus—unless the fraction really happens to be simple—it is best, when reporting probabilities or statistics, to use percentages.

There is a four-out-of-five chance the company will fail to release its next big innovation by the end of 2018.

There is an 80% chance the company will fail to release its next big innovation by the end of 2018.

There is a one-out-of-four chance that gas prices will skyrocket in the next month.

There is a 25% chance that gas prices will skyrocket in the next month.

Statistics show that roughly ten out of every hundred people are left-handed.

Statistics show that roughly 10% of people are left-handed.

Make *This* Clear

This is a word often used to refer to something mentioned in a previous sentence. However, using it in this manner can be imprecise.

While the meaning can usually be deduced from the context, you do not want something to be merely deducible, but rather self-evident. Specificity is the key to great writing.

Therefore, whenever using the word *this* to refer back to an idea, ensure that the reader is aware of the reference. If not, it may be better to simply restate the idea.

Unfair wages, imbalanced work opportunities, a chaotic labor market—this is what's wrong with society.

Society needs to address its unfair wages, imbalanced work opportunities, and chaotic labor market.

China is under fire for engaging in numerous private trade scandals, potentially jeopardizing its relations with global trade partners. If this continues, China might lose its long-standing reputation in international commerce.

If China continues to engage in private trade scandals, the country might jeopardize its relations with global trade partners and lose its long-standing reputation in international commerce.

The Ontario government has been criticized for its plans to remove sexual education from its provincial curriculum. For this reason, the next generation of Ontarians might have to ask their mothers for sex advice.

If the Ontario government follows through with its controversial plans to remove sexual education from its provincial curriculum, the next generation of Ontarians might have to ask their mothers for sex advice.

Prefer the Concrete to the Abstract

Unless you're writing a treatise on metaphysics, it is better to write in the concrete than in the abstract. Writing in the concrete allows readers to build a direct bridge between your ideas and their personal experiences. Prose that elicits a vivid picture in readers' minds is always superior to prose that merely goes to their heads.

Instead of forcing your readers to contextualize an abstract concept, why not contextualize it for them? Doing so is the essence of concrete writing. Therefore, if you wish to have your readers not merely understand but also retain what you say, be concrete!

His face shone with contentment.

He smiled broadly, his eyes filling with warm tears.

Fatigue ran through his body from head to toe.

His posture mimicked that of a weary old man.

Anger rushed through Charlotte's blood as soon as the revelation hit her.

Charlotte's face reddened, veins popping out, when her boyfriend said that he had been cheating on her.

Avoid Flowery Language

Flowery language is an unnecessarily elaborate way of writing. Many amateur writers will use pretentious language as a means of showing sophistication. This simply results in the opposite effect, making writers seem callow, insecure, and disingenuous. All writers' work will inevitably betray their character. Thus, it is both futile and immature to put on a facade, particularly one claiming higher knowledge than you truly have.

Flowery language, of course, has its time and place. For formal invitations and declarations, flowery language induces a sense of grandeur and stateliness that's impossible with plain, forthright English. Flowery language also often manifests itself in poetry, where writers can afford to have a more ornate writing style.

But these are special cases. As far as *transparent writing* is concerned, steer clear of flowery language.

He was baffled by the sheer immensity of her pulchritude.

He was surprised a woman could be so beautiful.

The extent of his equanimity was inconceivable.

He was extremely calm.

His capacity for circumlocution was unparalleled.

He could never give a straightforward answer.

Save the Best for Last

The Pareto principle is a general rule—applicable in all aspects of life—that states that, for any event, 80% of the effects arise from 20% of the causes.

The exact numbers themselves do not matter here. What matters is that most of the output in a given situation is determined by a small fraction of the input. In a basketball game, most of the points are scored by only a few players; in a company, a small portion of the employees yield most of the company's results.

Therefore, in alignment with the Pareto principle, roughly 80% of all the meaning derived from any sentence comes from 20% of the words. In other words, there are only a few words in any given sentence that convey the bulk of what it's trying to say. These are the *emphatic words* of a sentence.

If you place these words at the end of the sentence, even if readers have no clue what your sentence is about, they will at least know the object of its discussion. If they are reading a sentence that ends on the word *death*, readers will know, after finishing, that the sentence was somehow about death. Conversely, if you place the emphatic words in the middle, readers may have to perform mental gymnastics to find them.

David says **pizza** is his favorite food.

David says his favorite food is **pizza**.

John loves the **violin**, but he plays multiple instruments.

John plays multiple instruments, but he loves the **violin**.

The **emphatic** words of a sentence should be last.

The last words of a sentence should be **emphatic**.

PRINCIPLE 3

VARIETY

WRITING THAT LACKS VARIETY IS like food that lacks seasoning: Both are boring and unartistic. Although commonly overlooked, the principle of variety is indispensable in infusing flavor into your writing.

Diversifying your writing means giving it a sense of style and sophistication, resulting in a more pleasurable and stimulating reading experience while delivering your message with flair.

Vary Your Sentence Structures

Sentence structure plays an integral role in bringing rhythm to your writing. Consider the passages below: What makes them read so differently, despite the similarities in diction and theme?

Cathy ran to her room. She was tired and angry. She felt that no one understood her. She wanted only to fall asleep.

Cathy ran to her room, tired and angry. Feeling that no one understood her, she wanted only to fall asleep.

The difference lies in the two paragraphs' strikingly dissimilar structural compositions. The first paragraph possesses little structural variety, essentially being a series of short, evenly sized sentences with no special punctuation. As a result, the paragraph is lackluster and monotonous. The second version, however, has its own distinct rhythm, using commas and different sentence lengths to add spice and improve flow. Many writers tend to get too attached to a few familiar sentence forms. As a rule of thumb, unless done for rhetorical effect, avoid excessive repetition of sentences with the same syntax.

The Semicolon and Em Dash

The semicolon and em dash are infamous for their history of misuse in writing. When used improperly, they make your writing look amateurish and awkward. When used properly, however, they can enhance the presentation and flow of your writing.

Sometimes called a weak period, the **semicolon** is used to link two closely related ideas.

Ethan drives a BMW; Elsa drives a Tesla.

An **em dash** is an extremely versatile punctuation mark. It is typically used to interject subsidiary information into a sentence.

Elijah called his coworker—who happened to be on vacation at the time—to discuss their project proposal.

An em dash can also be used as a substitute for a colon.

Laughing, helping, empathizing—these are what defines true friendship.

Vary Your Paragraph Structures

When instrumentalists play in an orchestra, they tune their instruments in relation to the sound of the instruments around them. They pay careful attention to their roles in the orchestra Like instrumentalists, artistic writers will tune the length of a paragraph in relation to the lengths of those surrounding it.

While there is no ideal paragraph length—just as there is no ideal volume at which to play an instrument—as a rule of thumb, writers should aim to stay within a difference of two to three sentences between paragraphs to maintain balance in their writing.

However, it is also important to tailor the lengths of your paragraphs according to the role they play in driving forth your overall argument. While longer paragraphs are more explanatory, shorter paragraphs can pack more of a punch. A one-sentence paragraph, for example, can be extremely effective in emphasizing a fundamental proposition or idea, particularly if there are longer paragraphs preceding it.

Lingering Paragraphs

A lingering paragraph is an unnecessarily long, and therefore unsightly, paragraph. Consider the paragraph below. What do you notice about its structure?

The globalization of technology is becoming an increasingly prevalent issue in modern society. With the gravity of the issue comes a myriad of political and environmental matters that must be considered. Despite the multitude of wide-ranging benefits and resources technology has equipped society with, there are numerous negative repercussions that have come with the skyrocketing interest in technological innovation, especially for countries like Brazil. Brazil is the largest and most populous country in South America, with the ninth largest economy in the world. But despite its growing middle class and flourishing scientific prestige, Brazil faces many challenges, including rampant crime and corruption, poor infrastructure, onerous pensions, a restrictive business environment with strict labor laws that encourage a thriving black market, and a corrupt socioeconomic hierarchy. The ubiquity of technology necessitates an

> entirely new level of cybersecurity as well as other measures to combat its abuse. Brazil strives to leverage the power of modern surveillance mechanisms to help reduce crime, and has already begun doubling down on its cybersecurity architecture while simultaneously consolidating its emerging power status. Brazil, as a firm believer in technological advancement and its implications for eliciting positive change, holds the notion of a technologically-driven world at the core of its politics. The country aspires to collaborate with other countries to expand the scope of technology in relation to political matters around the world.

The first thing you probably noticed about the above paragraph was its wall-like construction. Perhaps you realized the content of the lingering paragraph could have been better divided into three smaller ones. Perhaps its length intimidated you enough to skip right down to this section. After all, massive bodies of text aren't particularly appealing to the eyes or the mind.

Readers simply cannot keep track of every idea being expressed in a thirty-sentence paragraph. They will lose themselves and have to reread, possibly multiple times. They'll wonder, "Is all this work worth it? Why can't the author be more organized?" It is therefore best to cut paragraphs into shorter chunks to make them easier to digest.

The best way to achieve digestible paragraphs is to plan them out ahead of time. Every paragraph should have a clearly defined theme. Ask yourself: "What am I trying to achieve with this paragraph? How does each sentence play into the theme? How does it fit into the broader scheme of the narrative?" By taking this kind of "first principles" approach, you will ensure that each paragraph is readable, structured, and purposeful.

Vary Your Word Choice

Word choice is vital in helping writers bring out their voice and style. Words, like paint colors, can shape the way a work is perceived. Bright, playful words can signal cheerfulness and optimism. Dark, serious words can signal gloominess and pessimism. Whatever palette writers choose to use will impact the message they are trying to convey to their readers.

Remember, however, that speculation alone will not help any writer determine the proper diction for their writing. The key is to experiment with different words to see how they affect the way your ideas are perceived.

Word Repetition

Variety is especially important for avoiding repetition and improving syntax in your writing. Compare the two passages below, paying attention to their respective flows.

Writing should not be seen as a task, but rather as a fulfilling activity. Why **should** that be the case? Because, by taking this approach to **writing**, your **writing** will improve as you will feel more motivated to **write.**

Writing should not be seen as a task, but rather as a fulfilling activity. Why? Because, by taking this approach, you will feel more motivated to write and improve as a result.

Keep an inventory of commonly repeated words, striving to replace them with fresh synonyms. The habitual use of identical words, especially when placed close together, dulls your writing.

PRINCIPLE 4

HARMONY

A WRITTEN WORK IS LIKE a piece of music: the chapters are the musical phrases, the paragraphs the chords, and the sentences the notes. If the composer wants to create beautiful music, the constituent elements must work together to form a unified whole, a whole greater than the sum of its parts.

The same is true of beautiful writing. The sentences, paragraphs—moreover, the propositions, arguments—must all operate in harmony for something beautiful to be made. The sentences in a paragraph must mutually agree just as the underlying assumptions in an argument must mutually satisfy. The slightest inconsistency, like the slightest musical dissonance, can throw off an entire audience.

Consider an internally inconsistent scientific theory. It postulates that (a) if P, then Q; and (b) if P, then not Q. Such a theory lacks harmony because its fundamental assumptions cannot logically coexist. Such a theory holds no weight. Likewise, a piece of writing that lacks harmony holds no weight. Harmony is what distinguishes a scholarly essay from an illogical series of words, a baroque fugue from a whining toddler's ruthless bashing of piano keys.

The importance of harmony is surpassed only by that of transparency. Without harmony, your piece is doomed to fail. If your sentences lack presentational elegance and your propositions lack compatibility, your writing lacks meaning.

Harmonize Your Language

Harmony of Language refers to the agreement between the linguistic units of a piece of writing.

Consistency of Voice

Imagine seeing a play in which, whenever the protagonist begins to sing, he changes his accent. It is easy to see why this is unacceptable: The actor isn't keeping in character. This abrupt inconsistency ruins the realism and professionalism of the performance.

The same type of predicament appears all the time in an inexperienced writer's work. The writer will begin in one voice and then change to a strikingly different one, using incompatible words, expressions, punctuation, and tone. Suddenly, the style will have shifted from upbeat and outspoken to solemn and introspective. This is jarring for readers because the writer is, like the unseasoned actor, not keeping in character. This predicament is further accentuated when the author decides to revert to their old voice later in their writing.

Switching between personas in your writing is amateurish and confusing to the reader. Ask yourself before engaging in any writing project: Who am I trying to be? What mode of speaking will best grip the reader in this case?

Presentational Elegance

Many writers overlook the importance of presentational elegance, that is, uniformity in spelling and typography. Just as it is important to focus on a written work's external presentation (its cover), it is equally important to focus on its internal presentation (its pages).

Why, then, do so many writers ignore this concept? Because the best works are those whose presentational elegance is invisible to the reader. While a poorly designed work is easy to spot, a work that has presentational elegance is rarely identified by the reader as such. The presentation of a work should only serve to enhance the reading experience. Therefore, a work's design must be omnipresent, but never conspicuous.

How does a writer achieve presentational elegance? Style guides (such as *The Chicago Manual of Style*) can help maintain a consistent presentational pattern throughout your writing and are widely accepted in the publishing industry. However, these style guides are not meant to be all-encompassing; they leave plenty of gray areas for writers to fill in.

Instead of dogmatically holding on to them, aim to tailor their preexisting guidelines to match your particular writing needs. In other words, create your own personalized style guide (of course without breaking too many rules): Include information about your preferred font sizes, line spacings, and spellings for words with more than one acceptable possibility. In doing this, you will bring a sense of consistency, harmony, and brand identity to your writing.

Parallelism

Parallelism harmonizes your ideas by repeating a chosen grammatical structure within a sentence or paragraph. Manifesting itself in the addresses of many of history's greatest orators, parallelism adds rhythm, balance, and symmetry in the expression of your ideas. Unlike consistency of voice and presentational elegance, parallelism is not essential to great writing, but rather an optional way to add emphasis.

In the following example, the entire sentence is an instance of parallelism.

Like father, like son.

The same concept can be used to create a parallel construction within a paragraph. Below is a passage taken from the second paragraph of Martin Luther King Jr.'s *I Have a Dream* speech—a prime example of parallelism between sentences.

> But one hundred years later, the Negro still is not free. One hundred years later, the life of the Negro is still sadly crippled by the manacles of segregation and the chains of discrimination. One hundred years later, the Negro lives on a lonely island of poverty in the midst of a vast ocean of material prosperity. One hundred years later, the Negro is still languished in the corners of American society and finds himself an exile in his own land. So we've come here today to dramatize a shameful condition.

Harmonize Your Thoughts

Harmony of Thought refers to the agreement between the logical units of a piece of writing.

Argumentative Coherence

Premises are the building blocks of an argument. In nonfiction writing, premises are the assumptions or points a writer makes. In fiction, they are the events that occur in a story. In both cases, premises lead to a final outcome, or conclusion.

An argument is the combination of a series of premises and the conclusion they entail.

An argument is said to be **valid** if the truth of the premises implies the truth of the conclusion—that is, the conclusion is a logical result of the premises. Here, it helps to distinguish between *truth* and *reality*: Truth is a property of premises and conclusions, whereas reality refers to the outside world. Therefore, a valid argument can have all *true* premises and an *unrealistic*—but still true—conclusion. (In fiction writing, of course, premises and conclusions are not necessarily realistic, but rather true and plausible *in the context of the story*.)

But why must we distinguish between truth and reality in the first place? Isn't it natural to assume that all true premises are also realistic ones? The problem is, many conclusions are taken for granted as being realistic simply because they agree with an argument's premises. But a technically valid—or structurally sound—argument is not necessarily one that describes reality! Worse, it may be persuasive and compelling but utter nonsense!

What does this all mean? As important as truth is, if all you care about in your writing is that the reader accepts your points, the only essential feature is *harmony* between the premises and conclusion of your arguments. This is the art of the politician. The seasoned yet corrupt politician knows that so long as your argument is coherent—that is, as long as the premises agree with each other and the conclusion agrees with the premises—it does not matter whether your premises, or supporting evidence, *are, in fact*, true.

Such deceptive writing cannot be considered artistic, for artistic writing leaves no room for dishonesty. Artistic writing places truth—truth that does not mold reality, but rather describes it—as its highest ideal. Artistic writing is not merely compelling writing. It is more than a means of persuasion—it is a means of persuasion to truth. The definition of truth, of course, is up for much debate. But so long as the writer writes what they believe to be truthful and righteous, the writer is writing artistically.

Unity

Unified writing sticks to a central theme. Anything that deviates from the primary theme must be struck out. Every argument, every proposition, every term must be made in direct relationship to the overarching theme of the writing. To write without unity is to sail without direction. No matter how far you go, you will never reach your destination. Consider the paragraph below. What makes it so *not unified?*

> Writing is an artistic pursuit, a means of self-expression. The artistic writer considers writing as playing a musical instrument: Each has both a technical and an emotional purpose. Writing that does not fulfill both criteria is not a work of art. Writing is a means of examining your life. Many would consider philosophy the ultimate study of the self. But before any progressive study can be done on the self, one must think, what is the self? Does it possess any concrete meaning or is it an entirely subjective construction? If one cannot define the self, how can one go about writing, given that knowing the self is a necessary component of artistic writing?

Although the above paragraph clearly does not lack in content, it is the lack of unity, the lack of direction, that makes it so frustrating and undecipherable. The reader is acquainted with one idea to start but gradually comes to be acquainted with a strikingly different one. This lack of logical harmony disrupts the flow of the reading experience. The writer is rapid-firing their thoughts, but none are hitting the reader. The writer has no control over their firearm, no control over how to logically order their premises. Thus, the writer wastes their ammo and misses their target.

Digression is the archenemy of the overzealous writer. Immature writers regard a piece of writing as an opportunity to divulge their personal convictions, constantly interjecting opinions when they have them. Writing is about prioritizing the reader, not the self! Never lose sight of your purpose in your writing. Doing so is the ultimate form of indulgence.

Say What You Mean and Mean What You Say

We have discussed Harmony of Language and Harmony of Thought. The interplay of these two harmonies is how we as writers communicate our ideas to readers. Harmony of Language and Thought describes the essence of effective communication: the agreement between your ideas and the linguistic elements used to communicate them.

For communication to be successful, what you say must refer to what you mean. If what you say is not what you mean, you have not communicated anything. And since the fundamental goal of writing is communication, lacking Harmony of Language and Thought in your writing is analogous to not writing at all.

CODA

MEDITATIONS ON WRITING

Reading to Write

Like any art form, artistic writing can only be achieved by studying its masters. Thankfully, most of history's greatest writers have left the world with their most prized teachings: their books. These are the books that fine-tuned the fabric of English prose, the books that have enlightened millions despite the wrath of time. By reading these books, you will come to gradually elevate your writing and your understanding of what it means to become an artistic writer.

How does one find these great books? I recommend studying the famous written works of our predecessors, from Homer's *Iliad* to Marcus Aurelius's *Meditations* to George Orwell's *1984*. What makes these books great is not merely their style of writing but also the profundity of their content. To write, you must have something to say. Therefore, to be an artistic writer, you must have artistic ideas. The best way to foster your artistry is to examine such books, both in style and in meaning. Beyond the classics, however, you should acquaint your self with the relevant books surrounding your interests. In this way, you may be able to write in a way that conforms to the norms of your subject matter.

Writing is not an independent process. It is not something that can be learned by locking yourself up in a room and practicing until your fingers bleed. Writing well requires exposure to the world. A well-written work is the product of the author's grasp of their environment. It is the product of what the writer knows, what the writer doesn't know; what the writer believes, what the writer doesn't believe. Everything the writer knows and believes is a product of culture. And culture is partially defined by the books that people have written and read.

The origins of culture lie in storytelling. Without the written wisdom of our forebears—from the pupils of Socrates to the disciples of Jesus—society would never have blossomed into what it is today.

Thus, the importance of reading in becoming a better writer is more than strictly practical. It is an obligation in the most profound sense of the word. To write is to contribute to society and culture. But before you can write, you must learn to read. Not all writing follows the rules outlined in this book—but the masters' writing styles, in essence, followed the same fundamental principles.

If you read great books, you will gain a fuller understanding of the world, which will, in turn, lead you to write great things.

Is There Objectively Good Writing?

Ironically, any answer to this question is intrinsically subjective.

One way of rephrasing the question is to ask, "Is there objectively good art?" While I don't believe that all art has an indefinite amount of equally qualified interpretations, the artistic merit of an artwork inevitably will vary depending on the viewer. In the reception of any work of art—particularly if it is doing well—lies an underbelly of criticism and disapproval.

However, there are factors that objectively enhance the quality of an artwork. There are paintings that are objectively better than others. Clearly, the *Mona Lisa* is objectively superior to a fifth grader's sketch of a stick figure. Clearly, Immanuel Kant's *Critique of Pure Reason* is objectively superior to a high schooler's philosophy essay.

I believe that objectively good art—and thus, objectively good writing—exists insofar as you can clearly differentiate it from objectively bad art. How do you differentiate objectively good writing from objectively bad writing? By using the principles in this book as your qualitative compass, you will be able to distinguish good writing from bad writing and improve your own writing style.

Time as a Valuable Resource

Time is simultaneously the writer's greatest gift and the writer's greatest burden. Time is what allows writers to write in the first place, yet it is also what most disheartens them. This is the wretched paradox that besets every writer, from businessperson to blogger. In a certain sense, time is a beast. It must be tamed so that it favors you and does not devour you. You must learn to treat it with kindness so that it follows you and does not prey on you.

Writing is like looking at yourself in the mirror over time. If you've made positive progress, you will feel content and continue writing. But if you've realized your progress has been subpar, you will feel unmotivated and go on a spree of self-resentment.

To become an artistic writer means to acknowledge that writing takes time and hard work. Writing is not for the impatient. It is a noble and creative pursuit. It is not something that can be learned in a matter of two weeks. Like mastery of a musical instrument, mastery of writing is a lifelong endeavor.

Planning Your Writing Sessions

Planning is the bane of all writers. Yet it is the best way to become a more productive and efficient writer. By planning your writing sessions, you will add order and structure to the writing process. Pinpoint times in your day where you feel comfortable putting everything aside to focus solely on writing. During these times, detach yourself from all external influences that may be gnawing at your attention. Wholeheartedly focus.

Write out the specific goals you desire to achieve in each particular writing session. In doing this, not only are you giving yourself a direction but also holding yourself accountable. The added sense of responsibility will enable you to write more quickly and easily.

Taking Breaks

One of the worst mistakes a writer can make in the writing process, apart from not writing at all, is trying to write too much. Many writers underestimate the importance of taking breaks during the writing process, staring fervently at glowing computer screens and ruthlessly bashing away at their keyboards. The issue with this approach is that, besides being detrimental to your health, you're not allotting yourself enough time to think. Writing is a slow process. Rushing will only result in a lousy piece of work.

Thus, a better (and more sustainable) approach is to take occasional breaks from your writing. These breaks can span from a few minutes to a few days to a few years. In these break periods, do not obsess over your writing. (Doing so would be self-defeating.) Instead, think of these breaks as a rebooting of the mind and body. You are restarting, renewing, refueling yourself, both mentally and physically.

If you adopt the practice of taking breaks, you will find that, upon revisiting your work, you will feel more motivated and driven. Furthermore, you will be able to see your work with fresh eyes—an invaluable aid for self-editing.

Writing as Autobiography

All written work, whether fiction or nonfiction, has a protagonist. In the former case, the protagonist is the character who carries the plot forward. In the latter case, the protagonist is the author. Now the author might retort, "But I can't possibly be considered a protagonist, for being a protagonist implies being a character." This is the fundamental difference between artistic writers and unskilled writers. Artistic writers consider themselves characters, whereas unskilled writers consider themselves writers—and nothing but writers.

As a writer, you must know that you, personally, are a constant presence in your writing. You are inextricably attached to your work. Your opinions and biases pervade your every sentence and paragraph. If you were to strip away your personality from your work while preserving all the same arguments and points, the work would no longer be yours. The expression, structure, and style of the writing would be so different as to be a distinct piece of writing.

After all, there are only so many new thoughts that humankind has come up with throughout history. Most writing, whether poem or thesis, story or commentary, is emulation. All writing is derivative, at least in its fundamental principles. To write, in other words, is to merely reinterpret what has already been written.

Every successful play has been based on precedent plays, every successful book based on precedent books. Every narrative follows a basic, universal plot structure.

This is not to defame or criticize humanity—I'll leave that to the politicians and nihilists—but to say that writing is necessarily autobiography. If a piece of writing is not an account of the writer's life, it is at least an account of the writer's character. All writers write for themselves no matter how selfless they appear to be. And unless this truth is acknowledged, those writers will forever remain immature and naive.

What distinguishes the best-selling book from the failing book is not the originality of the ideas, but rather how authors *express* the ideas, from *their point of view*. Thus, to write objectively is not only impossible but undesirable, for it removes the author from the work.

The Error of Arrogance

The precursor to becoming a master is the willingness to be a fool—that is, the willingness to make mistakes, embarrass yourself, and acknowledge your shortcomings. The writer who is unwilling to fail will never succeed, but the writer who is willing to fail will at least have a chance.

Arrogance is the downfall of the budding writer. Writers who exchange truth for pride, meaning for expediency, have only stripped themselves of all their artistry as writers and, moreover, as human beings. Enamored of their own intellect, they turn a blind eye to all that *can* be known, instead favoring that which is *already* known.

Artistic writers know that they are always insufficient. And it is precisely this insufficiency that motivates them to work harder and ultimately become better writers.

To be arrogant is to defy the fundamental goal of life: to become a better person. For how can you become a better person if you are already perfect?

The celebration of ignorance is the prerequisite to the acquisition of knowledge.

If you, as a writer, celebrate your shortcomings, you might someday come to celebrate your virtues.

Truth—the Cornerstone of Artistic Writing

Mutual trust is the precondition to meaningful social interaction. Before any conversation can be had, the interlocutors must necessarily agree to a mutual contract: that they will speak truthfully to each other.

The realization of this social covenant formed the basis for human interaction, predating even language itself. This shared sense of trust is what gave rise to primitive civilizations and the ethical codes that accompanied them. This foundational belief is what provided the original impetus for humanity's transformation from beast to human.

There is no more fundamental ethical tenet than this: that if I speak truthfully, I should expect you to speak truthfully. This notion of the requital of truth became the pedestal on which all subsequent moral principles were built.

What should happen, then, if this moral contract is breached? What should happen if when I speak truthfully to you, you lie in return?

When you put your trust in someone, you are inevitably making yourself vulnerable. You are giving away something you deem valuable to another individual. In doing this, you are also empowering that person to take advantage of you. The ultimate act of trust, therefore, is the ultimate act of faith.

If mutual trust is so essential to our being, how do we account for the ubiquity of "fake news" and the countless lies we hear every day? Why does false information seem to be so omnipresent, especially in magazines and news articles? How can authors be sincere to their readers in this age of gossip, media manipulation, and political pandemonium?

The world is a difficult place to alter. Most of the time, it is the world that is altering us. But if you stay true to yourself and that which you believe, and if you express it in your writing with the utmost passion and vigor, there is nothing but your own self-doubt to stop you from becoming an artistic writer. If there is nothing else in the world that you believe to be true, at least you know yourself to be true. This was the fundamental proposition established by the famous French philosopher and mathematician René Descartes, who declared, "Cogito, ergo sum"—I think, therefore I am.

Descartes himself was plagued with doubt, both in regard to his surroundings and the fabric of reality itself. Thus, he took it upon himself to discover the most basic proposition upon which he could rebuild his conception of life. By staying true to himself (and quite literally, only himself), he was able to thrive as a philosopher, mathematician, scientist, and writer.

If you act like René Descartes—that is, if you exercise freedom in thought and truthfulness to self—you, too, will flourish as a fount of knowledge, as an artistic writer. Your being is inextricable from your beliefs, anyway. So you might as well express them with the utmost truth.

Thus, as a final request of this book, I charge you with the task of only writing that which is truest and dearest to your heart. The four principles outlined in this book—economy, transparency, variety, and harmony—serve to help you write in a way that is truthful to who you are. By writing in any other way, you are doing a disservice to yourself and to the artistic ideal of truth.

ABOUT THE

AUTHOR

PETER YANG IS AN AWARD-WINNING writer, public speaker, and eternal student. Peter is currently working on a startup called Reviewerly, a user-generated content app that helps ecommerce store owners capture reviewers at checkout, set expectations from the get-go, and generate product reviews risk-free.

CONNECT WITH

PETER

Sign up for Peter's newsletter at
www.peteryangauthor.com/free

To find out more information visit his website:
www.peteryangauthor.com

Facebook Page:
www.facebook.com/peteryang854

Twitter:
peteryang854

Instagram
@peteryang_6641

LinkedIn
peter-yang-founder

BOOK DISCOUNTS & SPECIAL DEALS

Sign up for free to get discounts and special deals
on our bestselling books at
www.TCKpublishing.com/bookdeals

ONE LAST THING...

Thank you for reading! If you found this book useful, I'd be very grateful if you'd post a short review on Amazon. I read every comment personally and am always learning how to make this book even better. Your support really does make a difference.

Search for *The Art of Writing* by Peter Yang to leave your review.

Thanks again for your support!

Printed in Great Britain
by Amazon